FATHER JOHN DYER:

Colorado's Skiing Preacher and his Pioneer Roots

Rawlene LeBaron

2019

Portrait of Father John Lewis Dyer from his 1890 autobiography, *The Snow-shoe Itinerant.*

INTRODUCTION

The life of Father John Dyer is more than the story of an itinerant preacher skiing across rugged Colorado mountains to bring the message of the Gospel to pioneers and gold miners. His is the story of America – beginning with Father Dyer's great-great-grandfather, an indentured servant who came to this country, built a life, and was killed during the French and Indian War. His grandfather moved West with his family as the frontiers of Ohio were opened.

It was into this family of independent pioneers that Father Dyer was born on 16 March 1812. He settled in gold rush Colorado in 1861, fifteen years before Colorado became a state.

Isaac Beardsley in *Echoes from Peak and Plain* observed that

> *"Father" Dyer was never particular about where he preached whether in the street, saloon, cabin, school-room, church, on mountain, valley, or plain, so he delivered the message of salvation to dying men. In his preaching he never once considered ease, popularity, or salary. When taking a collection, he was always glad to get his hat back, if perchance there should be nothing of value in it, for he had spoken the truth to sinful men. What cared he whether he traveled on foot, horseback, or "snow-shoes!" The one burning desire was, that he "might not build upon another man's foundation."*

> *John L. Dyer has preached the gospel in more out-of-the-way places, and in more new towns, for <u>the first time</u>, than any other man, living or dead, within the bounds of the Colorado Conference."*

Rawlene LeBaron

This is his life.

COLONIAL BEGINNINGS

Roger Dyer
1705 - 1758
|
William Dyer
1728 - 1758
|
John Dyer
1757 - 1812
|
Samuel Dyer
1786 - 1871
|
John Lewis Dyer
"The Snow-shoe Itinerant"
1812 - 1901

Family tradition tells how Roger Dyer, Father Dyer's great-great-grandfather, slipped aboard an English ship and came to America as a stowaway. He was likely born in 1705 (Robin Propst Kile, *Hidden in the Mountains: Fort Seybert 1758*), making this about 1720 He was a penniless 14-year-old when he and some friends embarked on their grand adventure. The young English stowaways were discovered and "sold out" as indentured servants to pay their passage. Young Roger was lucky and "fell into good hands," a wealthy family who treated him well.

Whatever the details of his arrival in America, Roger Dyer likely immigrated as an indentured servant, like many who immigrated to America did during that time period. He soon worked off the cost of his passage and gained his freedom.

Roger married Hannah Smith, the daughter of William and Margaret (Hiatt) Smith Jr. of Cecil County, Maryland. Hannah's paternal grandparents were William Smith Sr., a large landowner in Cecil County, and his wife, Grace.

Soon after their marriage, Roger and Hannah Dyer moved to Lancaster, Pennsylvania, where their five children were born. They named their first child, a son born in 1728, William John Dyer, for Hannah's father, William Smith. A few years later, in 1731, their first daughter, Hester, was born. Their second daughter Hannah was born in 1734 and named for her mother. Then, Sarah was born in 1741, followed by James, born in 1744. It was a full household.

About this time, great tracts of the Virginia frontier extending all the way to the Mississippi River were opened up to settlers. Roger Dyer, his 20-year-old son William, and five other men, probably all of them from Lancaster, took advantage of the opportunity and bought tracts of land along the South Fork of the South Branch of the Potomac. Roger Dyer and his son William acquired a large tract of land, estimated at about 1,160 acres. On 5 November 1747, the seven recorded their deeds in the Augusta County courthouse. Over the next several decades, county lines would be redrawn, and by 1788, the South Fork Community, later called the Dyer Settlement, and still later, Fort Seybert, was in newly-created Pendleton County.

THE FORT SEYBERT MASSACRE

Settlers and Indians lived in relative peace along the frontier. . . for the time being. The Dyer Settlement grew rapidly, from the original seven families in 1747 to probably 40 families by 1758. During this decade, the four oldest Dyer children had married, and Roger Dyer and his wife Hannah had seven or eight grandchildren.

- William John Dyer, their oldest son, had married Margaret Hiatt about 1753. She was born in Orange County, Virginia, the daughter of John Hiatt Jr. and his first wife Rachel (Wilson) Hiatt, who had both immigrated from England. In 1754, William was commissioned Lieutenant of Foot in the Augusta County militia. They built a home on the land that William had bought and started a family. Their first son, Roger, was born in 1755 and named for his grandfather. Roger married Susannah Blizzard and served as captain of the Rockingham County, Virginia, militia during the Revolutionary War. He died in 1810 at Pendleton County, Virginia. About two years later, their second son, John Dyer, was born. Young John would grow up to be the grandfather of John Lewis Dyer.

- Hester Dyer, the oldest Dyer daughter, married Matthew Patton about 1749.

- Hannah Dyer married Frederick Keister about 1755. Born in Germany about 1730, Frederick had immigrated to America as a child on 24 September 1737 on the ship *Virginus Grace*. Hannah and Frederick may have had eight children: James, born 1756; Hannah, born about 1757; an unidentified daughter; Esther; Mary; Frederick Jr., born 1774; and George, born 1776. Frederick Keister was lieutenant of the Rockingham County militia and during the Revolutionry War was 1st lieutenant in the 46th Virginia Militia .

- Sarah Dyer, Roger Dyer's youngest daughter, was fair, with striking red hair and green eyes. She married Henry Hawes (alternatively, Haas or Hase) about 1753 or 1754, and they soon started a family. Henry died in 1755, leaving Sarah a young widow with a baby daughter, Hannah, named for her grandmother.

- James Dyer, the youngest child, was born 1744. He married Phebe Ann Harrison about 1767, Jane Ralston on 13 October 1780. and Nancy Jane Hall about 1797. He was a justice of the peace and credited with furnishing supplies for the American Revolution cause. He died about 1807.

The British and French were moving inexorably toward war. . . and the colonists and Indians would be right in the middle.The uneasy peace that existed between the British and the French/ Indian alliance was shattered on 28 May 1754 when the Battle of Junonville Glen in Pennsylvania, triggered the French and Indian War. The war was a conflict for empire, with the British and French with their Indian allies pitted against each other in North America. It would last until about 1763. The conflict spilled over to the European Continent, where it was known as the Seven Years' War.

George Washington was only 16 years old when he had helped survey the frontier Shenandoah Valley and understood the danger to this region. In 1753 he carried a letter from Virginia Governor Robert Dinwiddie to the French commander at Fort LeBoeuf. He hired Christopher Gist, agent for the Ohio Company, as a guide. During the trek, Washington explored the Ohio Country, gathered key intelligence for the British, and used his earlier surveyor experience to consider the most strategic fort locations. The French, he learned, were determined to control the Ohio Country, and the British could not depend on support from the Indians. In his letter, Dinwiddie told the French to leave lands along the Ohio River, which had been claimed by the British. While waiting for the French Commander's response, Washington detailed the dimensions of the fort, its defenses, and the number of large canoes. The French were strengthening their position and clearly were not planning to relinquish their hold on the Ohio Country.

The French defeated British General Edward Braddock at Fort Pitt in July 1755, exposing the western edge of Virginia, Pennsylvania, and Maryland to attack. That fall, both sides rushed to complete a series of forts.

In 1756, Jacob Seybert led the building of a small community fort, Fort Seybert, on his land to protect his family and his neighbors. This was next to Roger Dyer's land. Unlike the official forts built and garrisoned by the Virginia militia, Fort Seybert was barely 90 feet in diameter, a small two-story blockhouse surrounded by a circular stockade of vertical timbers about 12 feet high. The fort was built along the road that led to the old mill built by John Patton Jr., who had previously owned the land. It was about 100 yards from the mill and not far from the river's edge. Jacob Seybert was commissioned captain of the local militia in 1757.

In the spring of 1758, the Shawnee were on the move, and residents of the Virginia frontier were watching for signs of attack. On 27 April 1758, Shawnee raiders attacked a farming settlement along the west side of the South Branch of the Potomac. Most of the settlers fled to Fort Upper Tract, but after about an hour of resistance, the superior Indian force broke through the gate. The Indians massacred 23 people who had taken refuge in the fort – militia captain James Dunlap, 8 members of the militia, and 14 settlers. Young children disappeared, probably as captives. The fort was burned to the ground. Historians are divided on the role, if any, that French military advisors may have played in these attacks.

On the other side of South Fork Mountain, only about a dozen miles from the smoldering ruins of Fort Upper Tract, was Fort Seybert.

The morning of 28 April 1758 started quietly in the nearly deserted Dyer Settlement. Most of the men of the little farming community were members of the local militia and had gone to a neighboring settlement to protect it. Many of the women and children of the outpost had fled across Shenandoah Mountain to stay with neighbors. This included old Hannah Dyer, two of her three daughters and their children, daughter-in-law Margaret Dyer and her two sons, and her baby granddaughter, Hannah Hawes.   Those left behind had moved into the fort for safety. Houses were vacant, and the community was quiet, too quiet. A morning fog had settled in the valley, screening the Shawnee raiding party creeping up on the community.

This was not the same raiding party that had massacred the settlers at Fort Upper Tract. This band of about 40 to 50 Shawnee had moved down from Ohio and was led by Bemimo, known to the settlers as John Killbuck, a young chief eager to prove his success in battle and gain a reputation. He was the son of Netawatwees, a Delaware chief who had retreated from the Delaware Valley to Ohio as colonial settlements spread across the land. Killbuck hated the white settlers and was spurred by personal revenge. Years before, a settler named Peter Casey had offered a much younger Killbuck 14 shillings for catching and returning a runaway servant. Killbuck tracked and returned the servant, but Casey refused to pay him. Worse, Casey hit the proud Indian with his cane, knocking him to the ground. Killbuck never forgave Casey. Later, unable to exact revenge on Casey, he sought vengeance against all white settlers.

William Dyer, Roger Dyer's eldest son, was the first to be killed. He had gone out hunting early that morning, when he saw the raiding party. He attempted to fire on the raiders, but his flint-lock jammed. Virtually unarmed and defenseless, he was easily killed by the raiding party.

Roger Dyer's daughter Sarah, now the 24-year-old widowed mother of a young daughter, had started her chores early that morning. She planned to shear some sheep, and took with her young Wallace, probably an indentured servant. The two were caught by a pair of Shawnee. Sarah lashed out with her sheep shears, surprising one of the braves, and managed to push him down an embankment. While the second Indian laughed at the predicament of his companion, Sarah and Wallace fled to the fort and spread the alarm.

About 40 people, mostly women and children, were in the fort when the Shawnee attacked out of the morning mists. The settlers fought for their lives, returning fire and shooting the first two Shawnee to assault the fort. The settlers may or may not have heard of the massacre of their neighbors, but they were aware of other attacks. Seeking to quickly end the impasse, the Indian leader Killbuck spoke persuasively in English with Jacob Seybert. He promised that no one would be hurt if only the settlers gave up. If his raiding party had to take the fort by force, Killbuck threatened, the Shawnee would show no mercy. Everyone would be slaughtered. The settlers had a difficult decision. Many, even Seybert's 15-year-old son Nicholas, distrusted the Indians and fought against the surrender. In fact, Nicholas tried to shoot Killbuck, but was stopped by his father. In the end, the settlers gave up and walked unarmed out of the fort. They were mostly women and children, and this alternative, they thought, would save lives of those who would be unable to defend themselves.

The Shawnee ransacked the fort, took everything of value, and set fire to the timbers. Legends would later tell of a "lost treasure," valuables that the Indians stole, but had to hide when it slowed their retreat to Ohio. In some tales, the treasure is a half-bushel cache of coins in a copper kettle. In other tales, the nature of the treasure is unclear. Fort Seybert was a farming outpost on the frontier, and the treasure these hardworking families owned was their land and their livestock. Little material wealth is mentioned in the wills of those who were massacred. An inventory taken of Roger Dyer's estate included gold coins valued at 24 pounds and currency, but this was left behind by the Indians after the massacre. In all likelihood, any stolen treasure would have been metal tools and copper pots.

Killbuck's hollow promises soon proved to be only another weapon of war. The settlers were taken prisoner and marched a short distance toward the slopes of South Fork Mountain. Some of the settlers, fearing the worst, may have broken from the group as they were led away, but this, like so much of the family tradition coming out of this tragedy, cannot be proven. The Indians would keep as captives those who were strong and healthy and could contribute to the tribe. Others – the old, the weak, the handicapped – were seated on a large log, tomahawked from behind, and scalped.

This grisly practice of scalping was described by a French soldier, identified only as J.C.B, in his memoirs (J. C. B., *Travels in New France by J. C. B.*, ed. Sylvester K. Stevens, et. al.):

> *When a war party has captured one or more prisoners that cannot be taken away, it is the usual custom to kill them by breaking their heads with the blows of a tomahawk.... When he has struck two or three blows, the savage quickly seizes his knife, and makes an incision around the hair from the upper part of the forehead to the back of the neck. Then he puts his foot on the shoulder of the victim, whom he has turned over face down, and pulls the hair off with both hands, from back to front.... This hasty operation is no sooner finished than the*

savage fastens the scalp to his belt and goes on his way. This method is only used when the prisoner cannot follow his captor; or when the Indian is pursued. . . .

Both Jacob Seybert and Roger Dyer, then an old man, were tomahawked and scalped. When she saw her father murdered, Sarah fainted – this may have saved her life because the Indians believed that killing someone who had fainted would bring bad luck. Or, perhaps the Indians were impressed with the courage she had shown earlier when she fought back. Whatever the reason, she was taken captive rather than killed. Her younger brother, 14-year-old James, had been taken captive before the siege on the fort. With his black hair and dark brown eyes, it was hard to believe he was fair, red-haired Sarah's younger brother. He ran into the woods and nearly escaped, but a fast running creek blocked his path. It may have been his youth or possibly his speed as a runner that convinced his captors to spare him.

The Shawnee massacred 17 people at Fort Seybert, according to *The Preston Register*, a journal kept by William Preston, then clerk of the Augusta County Militia. (This register is now in the Lyman C. Draper Collection in the State Historical Society of Wisconsin.) The names of all the dead are not known with certainty, but some of the victims were Roger Dyer, William John Dyer, Jacob Seybert and his wife Elizabeth, probably John Reager and his wife Dorothea, and the boy Wallace. Jacob Seybert's mother Johanna may have been killed. Hannah Hinkle was "bedfast" and burned to death when the fort was set on fire. Another 24 people were missing, presumably taken prisoner.

On their return, the community was stunned at the death and destruction they found. They grieved and buried their dead in a common grave in the meadow several hundred feet from the ashes of their fort. In the 21st century, this common grave is a serene oasis surrounded by a stone fence, with only an embossed metal memorial reminding the visitor of the massacre that happened here:

Grave site of 17 Victims
of the Fort Seybert Massacure (sic)
April 28, 1758
Known Names
Cpt. Jaccob Seybert & Wife
Roger Dyer
Wallace Boy
William Dyer
Henry Haus
John Regger & Wife

The year before his death, Roger Dyer had written his will, naming his wife and children and expressing his love for his family. His will provides a glimpse into the lives of the Dyer family before the massacre.

In the name of God, AMEN: This twenty-fourth day of February in the year of our Lord, 1757, I, Roger Dyer of Augusta County in the state of Virginia, being weak in body but of perfect mind and memory, thanks be given to God, thereto calling to mind the mortality of the body, and knowing that it is appointed to all men, once to die, do make and ordain this to be my last will and testament, that is to say, principally and first of all, I give and recommend my soul in the hands of God who gave it and my body I recommend to the earth to be buried in a Christian manner, Executors nothing doubting, but at the Resurrection I shall receive the same again by the might power of God. And as touching such worldly Estate wherewith it pleased God to bless me in this life, I give, devise and dispose of them as follows:

***ITEM:** I give and bequeath to my well beloved wife Hannah Dyer, after debts and charges are paid, the full third part of all my movables, Estaid [estate] of goods and grants, whether in* *this Collony [Colony] or any other and one good bed and one good horse or mare which she shall use out of my stock, over and above the third part of the plantation I now live on [her "thirds" according to law], until my son, James Dyer, comes of age of twenty-one years, unless my wife marry again, then the plantation to be rented out for the use of my said son, James Dyer; I likewise constitute, make and ordain my well beloved wife my only and sole executor of my last will and testament.*

ITEM: I give and bequeath to my well beloved son, William Dyer, two shears [shares] to be equally divided between him and my three daughters after the rest is paid, what is nominated in this will and testament.

ITEM: I give and bequeath to my well beloved son James Dyer, the plantation I now live on [about 620 acres], with all the improvements thereunto belonging, and fifty acres serveyed [sic - surveyed] by itself, adjoining the same plantation I live on and not pattoned [sic - patented] as yet. Messauges [this term refers to the dwelling house, along with its outbuildings and adjacent land] and all profits thereunto belonging in anywise and fifty pounds current money with the said lands, to his heirs and assigns, forever.

ITEM: I give and bequeath to my beloved daughter, Hannah Gerster [Keister], a certain tract of land lying in Hampshire County consisting of 427 acres of land, more or less [Roger Dyer had bought this tract on 15 May 1755 from Enoch Cornwell], to her, her heirs, and assigns forever.

ITEM: I give and bequeath to my grandson, Roger Dyer, son of William Dyer, twenty pounds current money of Virginia. Now, after all of the above legacies are paid the remainder of my movables is to be divided into five parts and my beloved son William Dyer is to have two parts and my beloved daughters, Hester Patton, Sarah Hase [Hawes] and Hannah Gerster [Keister], each of them, one part. And I do hereby utterly disannul, revoke and

*disallow all and every other testament, ratifying and confirm-
ing this and no other to be my last will and testament; in witness
thereof I have hereunto set my hand and seal the day and year
above written.*

Signed and sealed in the presence of us:

Roger Dyer (Seal)

William Miller
Adam Hider[s]
William Gibson

Roger Dyer's will was proved and admitted to record the following year, on 16 May 1759 at the Augusta County Court in Virginia.

Following the Fort Seybert massacre, Killibuck and his braves
moved northwest to Ohio, taking their captives with them.
They knew that the colonial militia would not follow them into
the Indian strongholds. Among the captives were Sarah Hawes,
her brother James Dyer, and Jacob Seybert's six children: Nicholas, George, Henry, Elizabeth, Catherine, and Margaret. Also kidnapped were Mary Mallow and her infant daughter. When the
baby would not stop crying, the Indians brutally killed her. It
was a long, difficult trek, and the Indians relentlessly pushed the
captives. They finally reached Chillicothe, Ohio.

In June 1758, the Virginia militia patrolled the western frontier,
ending the Indian attacks on the settlements along the South
Fork.

After a few years of captivity, James Dyer was able to escape.
Charles Cresap Ward repeated the family tradition, passed down
by his great- grandmother, Elizabeth Dyer Ward, who died in
1891 (Talbot, *The Dyer Settlement; The Ft. Seybert Massacre*). James
was a fast runner, and the Indians often pitted him in races against
other white captives. The two would "run the gauntlet," racing
between two lines of Indians who would be whipping the runners
with switches and sticks, presumably to make the contestants

run faster. James later said that he always felt sorry for the other runner because he knew the other runner would lose. The loser would be killed, usually by tomahawking. According to family tradition, after a year and a half, James could no longer participate in these deadly gauntlet races. One day, during yet another life-or-death race, he simply continued running, and ran into the woods. The Indians followed, but James managed to elude them. When he saw a little house, he was so hungry that he took the chance to ask for food. An old woman welcomed him and fed him. Suddenly, his pursuers were at the door. The old woman quickly hid him in a storage chest, threw a pile of furs over him, and opened the door for the Indians to come in. The chief sat on the pile of furs as the braves looked around the little house. James later said that he was afraid the old chief would be able to hear the pounding of his heart. The Indians saw nothing to indicate that James was hiding there. As soon as the Indians left, James ducked out the door and continued his journey home. He swam the Ohio River and trekked though forests. He was able to reach his home in Virginia in about two weeks.

Sarah lived with the Indians for about three years before she was rescued. In some family traditions, it was her brother James who rescued her. More likely, it was her brother-in-law, Matthew Patton. Matthew Patton was taking his cattle to market when he heard talk of a red-haired woman living with the nearby Indian tribe. He soon confirmed that it was, indeed, the kidnapped sister of his wife, and he was able to rescue her. Sarah brought with her a beautifully carved spoon, the only memento of her hard life among the Indians.

Sarah was reunited with her daughter Hannah, her mother, and her sisters. About 1764, she married Robert Davis, and they had seven children: John, Samuel, Robert, Sarah, Elizabeth, Rachel, and Hester.

A year or two after the massacre, Nicholas Seybert was able to rescue his brothers and sisters. In 1768, he operated an inn in Fredericktown, Maryland, and later served in the Revolutionary War.

S. Key Dickinson retold a family story that his father, Demetrius Dickinson, had told him about a later reunion of Indian captives and their relatives (Talbot, *The Dyer Settlement; The Ft. Seybert Masacre*). Long after the French and Indian War, a party of Indians agreed to release their captives to waiting family members. A heartbroken mother came to the reunion field, looked at the line of captives, and could not recognize her daughter. The little girl was only four years old when she had been kidnapped by Indians 16 years earlier in the Fort Seybert area. Her name is not known, but she could be any unnamed child who was kidnapped during the conflict.

The mother turned to one of the officers overseeing the reunion. "How will I recognize my child? I know she's here, but she's a grown woman now, dressed as an Indian. She was only four years old when she was taken, how will she recognize me?"

The officer thought for a moment. "Do you remember the lullaby you sang to her as she was falling asleep? Can you sing it now?"

The mother was quiet for a moment, thinking of her lost child, and began singing the lullaby through her tears.

"Take a deep breath and try to calm down," the officer encouraged. "Sing to her in your normal voice, the voice she will remember."

The mother had barely started singing again, when a young woman broke from the main group of Indians. She was not standing with the other captives. "Momma! Momma!!" she sobbed, as she threw her arms around her mother.

THE MOVEMENT WEST

Following the Fort Seybert massacre, Margaret (Hiatt) Dyer was left a young widow with two sons, Roger and John, both under the age of three. She was named administratrix of William John Dyer's estate on 17 August 1758, and his estate was finally settled the following year, on 5 December 1759.

On 20 February 1759, Margaret Dyer married (2) John Cravens (his name also appears as Craven in some records), who had been born in Sussex County, Delaware. In 1765, John Cravens was named guardian for his two stepsons, "Roger and John Dyer, orphans of William Dyer."

In addition to Roger and John Dyer, Margaret and John Cravens had seven children: Mary, Hannah, Robert, William ("Billy"), Joseph, James, and Margaret. In his autobiography, Father Dyer recalls Reverend Billy Cravens, his great uncle, as "a Methodist, fearless and determined, dealing still-houses and dram-drinking fearful blows, and certainly the boldest anti-slavery man of his age." It is easy to see that the larger-than-life pastor could beome a role model for the impressionable youmg John Lewis Dyer.

About 1780, John Dyer married Jane Morrel. Their first three children -- Mary, William, and Samuel – were born in Pendleton County, Virginia. In the spring of 1788, two years after young Samuel was born, the Dyer family moved west, the first of several moves. John's brother Roger decided to remain in Pendleton County. The family settled in Kentucky, about six miles from Lexington. Ten years later, in 1798, the family moved again, northward to Station Prairie, Ohio, then a stronghold against Indians. This was near Chillicothe, where James Dyer and his sister Sarah had been captives of the Shawnee years before. In 1800, three years before Ohio was admitted to the Union, the Dyer family moved again, this time to Pleasant Township, Franklin County, Ohio, where John Dyer built the first gristmill in Central Ohio. The area was then known as Dyer's Mills.

A frequent visitor to the Dyer household was Reverend Lewis Foster, a traveling Methodist preacher. His father, John Foster, also a Methodist preacher, had served in the Revolutionary War from Maryland in the company led by Captain Peter Mantz.

No one was surprised when young Samuel Dyer fell in love with Cassandra Foster, the daughter of Reverend Foster and his wife, Ann (Davis) Foster. They were married on 4 October 1810 at the Foster household in nearby Madison County, Ohio.

Born a few months after John Dyer's death, John Lewis Dyer never knew his pioneer grandfather. Growing up, he heard family stories about his grandfather, whom he termed "quite a character." In addition to his gristmill, John Dyer built a sawmill. In one anecdote that Father Dyer repeated in his autobiography, John Dyer sawed into planks a particularly fine cherry log. These cherry planks, he said, would be used for his coffin, and he stored them in the loft of his home. When John Dyer died on 12 January 1812, he was buried, as he had planned, in a coffin crafted from those cherry planks. Reverend Foster officiated at the funeral of his old friend.

When John Dyer wrote his will on 7 January 1812, he anticipated his own death a few days later. He was only 55 years old.

> *I do hereby will all my estate real and personal to be settled according to the laws of the State of Ohio, but my grist mill and sawmill and as much land as lies with the barn as described: Beginning a white [illegible] on Big Darby marked with the letter "D: and thence to a white oak on Little Darby a line tho [sic] west of the dam marked D containing fifty acres more or less and to be sold by Jane Dyer, my loving wife and William Dyer, my loving son and when the above-described mills are sold according to*

the payments it is to be divided equally between William Dyer, Mary Reed, my loving daughter, Samuel Dyer [the father of John Lewis Dyer], Robert Dyer, John Dyer, Morrel Dyer [named for his mother's surname], Joseph Dyer, my loving sons and daughter. In witness whereof I set my hand and seal this 7 day of January 1812.

> *John Dyer*
> *Alex Blair*
> *John Turner*
> *Proved and ordered to be recorded March 22, 1813*

Samuel Dyer and his bride Cassandra (Foster) Dyer settled on a farm near his father's old mill at the junction of the Darbys in Franklin County, Ohio. From 1815 to 1821, Samuel Dyer was the local justice of the peace.

John Lewis Dyer, named for both his grandfathers, was born 16 March 1812, the first of their nine children. The other children were:

- Robert C. Dyer. He was born about 1814 and died in a gun accident about 1855.
- Rebecca Dyer. She was born 1816 and married Harvey Foster.
- Thomas Dyer. He was born 1819 and married Mary Foster. He died in a well accident 1866.
- Rachel Dyer. She was born 30 May 1821. John Lewis Dyer later officiated at her marriage to Dr. Wilson B. Thurston at Platteville, Wisconsin, on September 1855.
- Jane Dyer.
- Ann D. Dyer. She was born 1828 in Ohio and married William Bailey.
- Elizabeth L. Dyer.
- Joseph Dyer. He was born 1833 in Illinois.

JOHN LEWIS DYER

John Lewis Dyer and Harriet Foster were married on 4 December 1833 in Canton, Illinois. She was the youngest daughter of Zebulon Foster and his wife, early settlers of Cincinnati, Ohio, then Fort Washington, who had migrated west to Illinois. John Dyer's oldest sister Rebecca married Harriet Foster's brother, Harvey, linking the two families even closer.

When the Panic of 1837 financially devestated the growing nation, John had a wife and two young children: Joshua, born in 1834, and Elias, born in 1836. The crisis lasted into the mid-1840's. In his autobiography, John Lewis Dyer recalled

> *From 1834 to the spring of 1837, times were good, and speculation ran high. But the awful crash financially, in 1837, broke up thousands. Only men that had a surplus of money and were out of debt, stood the shock. No money could be had on credit for less than twelve per cent, and property and produce were not worth anything to speak of. I hauled one load of good wheat thirty-five miles to Peoria, and could get only twenty-five cents a bushel. Pork was sold from $1.25 to $1.50 a hundred pounds. The farmer had to run all over a village to sell a few pounds of butter at six cents a pound, and take it in calico. Eggs were three cents a dozen.*

In 1844, John and his growing family moved to Potosi, Wisconsin, where he was a lead miner and prospector.

Harriet Dyer died in Potosi on 14 July 1847, a loss that nearly crushed him. Then, six weeks later, John was again grief stricken when their youngest daughter, thirteen-month-old Harriet, died on 8 September 1847. Mother and daughter were buried next to each other at Van Vuren Cemetery in Potosi, Wisconsin. John was now a widower with four children; Joshua, 12; Elias, 10; Abbie, 7;

and Samuel, 4.

Reflecting on his emotional and financial troubles, John relied on his faith. Surely, he prayed, "the Giver of all good gifts would help in the hour of distress." Very soon, he struck a vein of mineral worth several hundred dollars, This would alleviate at least some of the worry and uncertainty in his life.

Looking back, he had no plans to marry again. Five months after Harriet's death, however, John was lonely and determined to marry again. It was much too soon and proved to be disastrous. Sarah Whiting, a widow who lived nearby, accepted his proposal, and they were married on 14 December 1847. Sarah Whiting's second husband had died, making her a widow, but John soon discovered that his bride was never divorced from her first husband, a man who was still very much alive. He felt he had disgraced himself with his family, his friends, and his faith by living as the husband of a woman who was already married. Within a year, he got a divorce. In his autobiography, John Dyer mentions that Sarah, "my divorced woman," died in a sudden flood in 1851. "Poor, unfortunate woman! if she had remained in her house, the sad occurrence would not have happened." He never refers to her by name.

He needed to get away from the public humiliation and laughing eyes. He soon moved his family from their home in Potasi, Wisconsin, to Lost Grove, a community near Mineral Point, Wisconsin, where he could continue prospecting for lead.

In 1850, John Dyer was counted in the census working as a miner and living in Linden, Wisconsin, with his brother Robert, also a miner, and their sisters, Elizabeth and Rachel, and his children – Joshua, 15; Elias, 12; Abbie (Elizabeth in the census), 10; and Samuel, 7. It was a full, active household.

When his younger sister Rachel offered to care for the children, John was able to fulfill his dream of becoming a Methodist itinerant preacher in Wisconsin and Minnesota. He was concerned by what he felt was his lack of schooling and would later ensure that all four of his children received a good education. As he later mused in his autobiography, "My own advantages had been limited, but I coveted the best things for my children."

In 1851, he was admited to the Conference at Waukesha, Wisconsin, and preached as a "ciruit rider" until he moved to Denver in 1861. Life as a circuit rider was difficult – low pay, dependence on a kindly parishoner for food and lodging, and travel, travel, travel across a circuit that would six weeks to cross it. As a very family-oriented man, he likely saw the biggest hardship would be being away from his family.

In 1855, John's younger brother Robert was fatally wounded when a gun he was resting on a door step accidentally "discharged into his side, near his vest-pocket, ranging up into his stomach." Robert died 36 hours later. Robert was only two years younger than John, and they had been very close. Praying for God's help to bear his anguish, John Lewis soon returned to preaching two or three times on Sunday, with other appointments during the week.

In Seprember 1855, John Dyer officiated at the marriage of his sister Rachel to Dr. Wilson Thurston.

As soon as the snow melted in February 1856, John moved his family to Minnesota. He recalled crossing the "Wisconsin and Mississippi on the ice at Prairie du Chien." Near Lenora, he worked on clearing the campground, platting the 40 acres, and took two lots as payment instead of the $50 offered. In his autobiography, John reports his failed efforts to build a simple stone church:

> *Our part of the country was filling up fast with settlers, and we set in to build our church of stone; but the walls were not nearly up when cold weather came. Then followed the spring of 1857, and with it the financial crash. This was much worse here, from the fact that we were all new settlers. The majority*

of the people had spent most, if not all, that they brought with them, and had not time as yet to make anything off their farms. There was scarcely any money in the country; and land that had been bought from the government at one dollar and twnty-fove cemts, could not be sold for that much, including the improvements. Nothing was at par, save the salvation of our souls.

With $1,600 that he managed to save, John bought 200 acres and established a home for himself and his two younger children: 15-year-old Abbie and 12-year-old Samuel. The Panic of 1857, the first worldwide financial crash, would severely impact him. With others, he had offered security for a man to set up a sawmill in the community. When the venture failed, the father of the failed businessman foreclosed on 38 acres of John Dyer's land. Making matters worse, John Dyer, even though he was responsible for two children, was regarded as a single man and paid $100 a year quarterage. "Suffice it to say," he remarked in his autobiogrphy, "I was financially burst; actually sold my mule to pay a debt, and started on foot to my circuit."

"PIKE'S PEAK OR BUST!"

It was the ninth of May 1861 when John Lewis Dyer started his journey to Colorado to see Pike's Peak. He thought he was going blind and depended on a patent medicine to open his eyes every morning. If he wanted to see Pike's Peak, he needed to go now. He was nearing his fiftieth birthday and had little to keep him in Minnesota.

His wife Harriet had died almost 14 years earlier, on 14 July 1847, in Potosi, Wisconsin, and his four children were now grown and leading their own lives.

Elias Foster Dyer, his middle son, born 8 October 1836, had moved to Colorado the year before, drawn by the recent gold strikes. He worked as a clerk in Mr. Sprague's general store in West Denver and prospected for gold when he could find the time. John Dyer missed his son and looked forward to being with him. Elias had not yet volunteered to serve during the Civil War because he frequently used a cane, the result of "white-swelling" when he was 15 years old.

His other two sons, now adults, would both volunteer with the Union Army in the Civil War. Joshua, born 8 October 1834, was almost 27 years old, and young Samuel, named for his grand-father, was 18 and a student at Galesville University, a private college in Gatesville, Wisconsin, that would be formally oper-ated by the Episcopal Methodist Church. Joshua first enlisted with the 1st Minnesota Infantry on 5 November 1861. On 14 August 1862, Samuel would enlist with Company K, 5th Wisconsin Infantry. Both enlisted after their father had moved to Colorado.

His daughter Abbie was almost 20 years old. She had dropped

out of Hamline University after a term to marry Charles Clinton Streeter. Now a young mother, Abbie lived in Lenora, Minnesota, with her husband and baby daughter, Harriet Louella Streeter, born 26 August 1860 and named for her maternal grandmother, Harriet (Foster) Dyer.

With $14.75 in his pocket and a few possessions, he left Lenora, Minnesota, that morning, heading toward Omaha. He often walked and considered himself lucky to have a "splendid riding animal" for this journey.

He thought of his accomplishments over the past six years in Minnesota. In many communities, he had been the first preacher and had helped form religious societies. He lost count of the number of people he had ministered to, but he estimated there were over 500. He then thought of his financial condition, and everything he had pledged to build a church. His church. It was never finished and lay in ruins, a symbol of his stillborn dreams. (His church, the Lenora Methodist Church, was rebuilt in 1865, years after he left. The dedication plaque reads, "In memory of Rev. John L. Dyer, first pastor, and other pioneer Methodist preachers and church members of Southern Minnesota.") There was no way out. Even after giving up nearly everything he owned to repay loans, he still owed about $700. This was a huge debt for a poor preacher. After a lifetime of hard work – mining, farming, and preaching – what did he have? He left town nearly penniless, committed to making a fresh start in the gold fields near Denver. He would somehow repay what he owed. His dream of building a church was perhaps only delayed.

He traveled 47 miles that first day, his thoughts of the past alternating with his hope for the future, on the long ride. That night, he stopped with someone he slightly knew. In the morning, Dyer asked for his bill, and his acquaintance "looked down his nose, and said, 'Twenty-five cents.'" The insult was still sharp in his mind 30 years later when he wrote his autobiography.

He kept a steady pace, averaging 50 miles a day until he reached Newton, Iowa. There, because of the carelessness or selfishness of his innkeeper, his horse nearly died. He fed and attended to his horse and then went to breakfast. When John Dyer returned to the stable, he found that the innkeeper had moved his horse to a different stall to avoid disturbing a sitting hen. A half-bushel of corn was in the new stall, and when his horse ate it, she got so sick she nearly died. All this to avoid upsetting the hen! His horse could not go on, and John was forced to trade her, along with saddle and bridle, for what he could get. The trade was an uneven one. He settled for $15 in cash, a gun, and an old watch.

He walked the rest of the way to Colorado.

At Omaha, he paid $15, half the money he had, to join Mr. Penny's 18-wagon train that was going to Pike's Peak. The train would carry his belongings, but he would have to walk the 600 miles across "the American Desert." The long, exhausting trek was comparatively uneventful. They met with the occasional Indian, but they were never threatened. John was disappointed that he never spotted a buffalo, "much less a chance to shoot one." It was Thursday, the twentieth of June 1861, when John Lewis Dyer arrived near Denver, two miles up Cherry Creek. Colorado. He would build a new life here.

He gathered up his few belongings, only to discover that his pocketknife and pouch with all his money had been stolen. Penniless, he walked to Denver to meet his son, Elias.

SETTLING IN COLORADO

John Lewis Dyer spent his first few days in Denver with his son, Elias, catching up on events of the past year and walking around the city.

The 1861 census for Denver showed a population of about 3,000. The official Colorado Territory Census results were published in September 1861:

White males over 21 years of age	18,136
White males under 21 years of age	2,622
Females	4,484
Negroes	89
Total	25,331

The disappointing census reflected a decline in population from the year before. Many of the gold seekers from "the States" had become disillusioned and returned home, broken and weary. Others left the Colorado gold fields to enlist in the Civil War. The state was split: some fought for the Union, others for the Confederacy. This was an explosive topic in a divided territory, as John Dyer would discover.

John Dyer eagerly read *The Rocky Mountain News* his first evening in Denver, Thursday, the twentieth of June 1861. The advertising and brief local news in the four-page daily newspaper echoed the vitality and excitement of early Denver. Merchants advertised groceries and mining supplies, bankers and dealers in gold dust offered coins in exchange for gold dust. The many storage and commission agents competed for advertising space. Freight lines boasted their schedules. Harrison and Co. of Mountain City announced they had acquired 200 barrels of "pure rye whisky" and imported brandies, enough to furnish the hotels and saloons of Denver. A "Grand Fancy Dress Ball" was planned on the Fourth of July to mark the grand opening of the National Theater at Central City. The Nevada House at Nevada City (today, Nevadaville is a ghost town near Central City) invited the general public to another Fourth of July Ball. A cryptic block notice warned: "Beware of Apex Road." The latest news spanned the quartz yields at Gold Hill and such brief personals as:George M. Pullman, of Central City, arrived last evening, from the mountains en route for the States (Colorado would not be granted statehood for 15 years). He has with him a collection of the most beautiful specimens of nuggets and gold-bearing quartz we have ever seen, obtained, most of them, from the Fisk lode. Mr. Pullman leaves in Saturday's coach for the east.

John Lewis Dyer later met William Newton Byers, editor and publisher of The Rocky Mountain News, at his printing office in Denver. Byers had arrived in Denver on the 21st of April 1859, bringing a printing press and a wagonload of newspaper supplies. His fledging newspaper, first published two days later, on 23 April 1859, soon became the voice of the Rocky Mountains. It was published for almost 150 years, ceasing publication on 27 February 2009. John remembered that Byers had been born in Madison County, Ohio, and the two men had briefly lived within a few miles of each other. The Byers-Evans House that William Byers built in 1883 in Denver, is now a museum open to the public.

John was intrigued by the Denver ten-dollar gold pieces. Clark, Gruber & Co. had opened a coinage mint in Denver at the corner of 16th and Holladay (now Market Street) streets the year before, on 20 July 1860. Their ten-dollar gold pieces, minted from the pure gold from area mines, were engraved with an image of Pike's Peak and the legends "Pike's Peak Gold," "Denver," and "Ten D" for the ten-dollar denomination. On the reverse the legend "Clark, Gruber & Co." encircled an American eagle, with the "1860" date. Thousands of these gold coins were minted. This was the only gold coinage mint established in Denver, but some of the mountain mining towns had their own mints. John Parsons' mint in Tarryall, for example, stamped out $2.50 and $5.00 gold pieces. About two million dollars in gold was produced in Tarryall before the mines "played out," and by 1875 the once-boisterous, hard-drinking boom town was deserted.

John Dyer met Reverend Walter Kenny, the preacher for the Methodist Episcopal Church in Denver, who invited him to preach on Sunday evening. He spoke on repentance and the unconditional surrender of the Confederacy, a controversial topic in Denver in June 1861. Just a few months earlier, on 12 April 1861, Confederate forces had fired on Fort Sumter, triggering the American Civil War. Colorado was split, with half the state supporting the Union and half supporting the Confederacy.

John Dyer had said in his autobiography that he wanted to see Pike's Peak, but he did not go there. Instead, he quickly made plans to go to the gold mining camp of Buckskin Joe. He wanted to return to Denver by the end of September. He had heard tragic stories of travelers and prospectors trapped in the mountains by avalanches and early winter snows. In the winter of 1848, 11 men and 120 mules in John Fremont's party died trying to find a route over the San Juan Mountains for the Pacific Railway.

He traded his watch for about $20 in provisions. He later calculated that his supplies – coffee, sugar, flour, bacon, canned fruit, and salt -- cost about $.25 a pound. His son Elias gave him a buffalo skin and quilt.

By the third of July 1861, he was ready. A company with a team would carry his belongings, and he would walk the hundred miles to Buckskin Joe.

The trek took seven days. On the ninth of July 1861, he reached Buckskin Joe, a turbulent mining town in the shadows of Mount Lincoln. The mining town was named after Joseph "Buckskin Joe" Higgenbottom, a flamboyant mountain man known for his rough-sewn leather clothes. Buckskin Joe, one of six prospectors in the area in September 1859, claimed that he made the first gold strike here. Records show that it was Hart Harris who discovered gold a year or so earlier while deer hunting. Hart shot at a large buck. He thought he missed his target, but he looked at the ground for traces of blood, anyway. Perhaps he wounded the deer. He stared at the dirt, astonished by the unmistakable glitter of gold. His bullet had struck a lode of rich placer gold.

In 1860, Jacob B. Stansell, Miles Dodge, and J.W. Hibbard platted out a town. Like many mining towns, Buckskin Joe had a succession of names. It was first called Buckskin Joe, then formally named Laurette, a combination of the names of the wives – Laura and Annette – of the Dodge brothers. This name soon was changed back to Buckskin Joe. A stamp mill was built to process ore from the Phillips Lode. Soon, 24 stamp mills and about a dozen arastras were built to process area ores. Arastras were rude circular stone mills that crushed ores with heavy stones hanging by ropes from a pole.

By 1861 Buckskin Joe was one of the most exciting boom towns in the Rocky Mountains, "the bonanza of the country." Oro City was "played out," so many of the prospectors and storekeepers, including Horace and Augusta Tabor, moved to Buckskin Joe. Horace Tabor filed some mining claims in the area and bought about 20 additional claims, but none were productive. It was their general store, run primarily by his wife Augusta, that supported the Tabor family during the early years.

With the growing demand for lodging, hotels popped up like great mushrooms after a spring rain. Soon the town boasted Fitzgerald's O.K. House, Gibson's Lauret House, Mrs. Green's Cherokee Hotel, and the St. Charles Hotel. Downtown Buckskin Joe echoed with music, laughter, and noise from three dance halls and a theater. Jacob B. Stansell, one of the town's founding fathers, funded a black minstrel company that performed regularly. Theatrical troupes entertained large, boisterous audiences. That fall, a post office was established in Buckskin Joe.

It was to this rough mining camp that John Dyer came. The year before, Reverend William Howbert had presided over a funeral, and Brother William Antis had held a service, but these were one-time events. That Sunday, John Dyer helped select a shady location with fallen logs for seating so they could hold an outdoor service. Reverend Howbert, now on the South Park Mission, preached, and John Dyer volunteered. About 20 people participated in the first class.

John Dyer was encouraged. He settled into a small pole cabin thatched with pine boughs and decided to extend his work to the neighboring communities. This would be his home for the next nine weeks. He planned to preach in all the small neighboring mining camps that were within walking distance.

On the first Sunday in August, he walked eight miles to Montgomery, a mining town at an altitude of 10,783 feet, to preach to the miners. There, he was invited to eat and talk with one of the men. Then, he walked on to Quartz Hill, a mining camp at the timberline, and preached to about 30 attentive miners. He walked 16 miles back to Buckskin Joe, where he held two services that evening.

The following Sunday, he walked to Fairplay, where he preached the first sermon in that mining camp. Fairplay was a boom town settled in 1859 by gold prospectors who had been turned away from Tarryall by miners who refused to share their luck – even though there were more claims than they could work. In Fairplay, John Dyer had an attentive audience of about 30.

On Friday, 16 August 1861, he preached his first sermon in Mosquito. There were no houses, so he preached by a campfire.

The Oro City preacher, H.H. Johnson, had asked John Dyer to replace him and assured him that all arrangements had been made for the transition. However, Dyer soon discovered that Johnson had left in disgrace. The log church in Oro City had been destroyed. Worse, Johnson had not informed the presiding elder of the Rocky Mountain District of the Kansas Conference, then Col. John M. Chivington, that Dyer would be taking over this mission.

John M. Chivington had arrived in Colorado the year before, on 19 May 1860. Frank Hall reports that "he began at once with irresistible energy to institute a thorough system of church work," and soon applied this energy to military and political advancement.

Because John Dyer did not have an official appointment, he would receive no financial support from the church. He estimated that he had only six or seven church members scattered across a hundred miles of rugged mountain wilderness. He would need to depend on his own resources.

On 16 September 1861, he set out for California Gulch, a booming gold camp that grew into the town known today as Leadville.

When Abe Lee found gold in California Gulch the winter before, he triggered a gold boom. He and some other Georgia prospectors were panning in the Arkansas River. They had tried their luck at Russell Gulch and then moved on to Cashe Creek. Snow was on the ground, and sand in the creek bed was frozen. Everything seemed hopeless. Then, Lee saw the unmistakable glint of gold on the bottom of his pan.

"I got it! I found it!" Lee shouted. "It's the whole State of California in the 'God damn pan.'"

John Dyer hiked eight miles to the top of Mosquito Pass, looked across the spectacular landscape, said a prayer, and continued on his way. That evening, he preached at California Gulch, and in the following months preached at many of the area's mining camps -- Washington Gulch, Kent's Gulch, Georgia Gulch, Fairplay, Buckskin Joe, Minersville.

In his autobiography, John Dyer remembered passing through Deadman's Gulch, named for the six white men killed by Indians in 1859. The bones of these six men and their horses, bleaching in the sun, had been uncovered by wolves and now marked the old trail. As travelers passed by, they shuddered and imagined the ghosts of the dead wailing through the pines and spruce . . . but no one stayed to rebury the bones.

To supplement the erratic collection plate – he received about $43 – he worked during the day.

He had been a successful lead miner in "the States" and looked forward to prospecting for gold in what was now one of the richest gold mining regions in the world. He partnered with Noah Armstrong, and the two men bought a jack and supplies. They prospected for about three weeks. They were unsuccessful, but continued prospecting until the snow fell, catching them 70 miles from winter quarters. Snow reached five feet deep, and it took them three and a half days to go as many miles. They finally reached California Gulch.

For ten nights, John Dyer held prayer meetings in the schoolhouse, until the townspeople wanted the building for a community dance. Dances would be Father Dyer's lifetime *bete noire*, an activity that he despised, one that he was convinced competed for men's souls. In his autobiography, he clarified his views on dancing:

> *I have for many years thought that dancing causes more of the evils in society throughout the nation, than any other institution the devil ever started; but that if it were done without music, and men and women danced by themselves, it would not do much harm.*

On 7 January 1862, he started for Buckskin Joe. At Weston Pass, a treacherous mountain pass named for Algernon Weston, he was caught by a snowstorm. He wrote in his autobiography of wading through waist-deep snow, and after five or six hours he was nearly exhausted. When he could no longer go on, he decided, he would write his own epitaph on a pine tree: "Look for me in heaven." Finally, about an hour after dark, he stumbled his way to safety.

He walked to Fairplay, and then on to Buckskin Joe. For two weeks, he held prayer meetings, meetings that were successful despite what he considered "every kind of opposition – at least two balls a week, a dancing-school, a one-horse theater, two men shot." He considered dancing in the same class as killings.

The first week in February 1862 he returned to Denver. The weekly stage to Denver cost ten dollars, so he decided to walk. "If I did not make money," he reasoned, "I could save some." It took him two and a half days.

Looking back, he estimated that he walked about 500 miles during those months in the mountains and preached about three times a week. He received no payment from the church. His clothes were dirty and torn, and his shoes were partially resoled with rawhide. His hat rim was patched with antelope hide. He did not have a vest. He had lost about 30 pounds since leaving his home in Minnesota and now weighed a lean 163 pounds. Despite his shabby appearance, he was fit and healthy, his eyesight had improved, and he was optimistic about the future.

As he walked into Denver, he looked more like an unlucky prospector than an itinerant Methodist preacher from "the States."

RETURN TO THE MOUNTAINS

Back in Denver, John Dyer learned of a Saturday night prayer meeting and quietly slipped into a middle row to listen to the preacher. The preacher, wearing a military uniform and carrying a bowie knife and revolver, was the former Methodist presiding elder, Reverend John M. Chivington, now Major Chivington of the First Regiment of Colorado Volunteers. In November 1884, Chivington would lead his troops, 700-strong, against a peaceful village of Cheyenne and Arapaho in what became known as The Sand Creek Massacre. Chivington and his troops killed at least 70 – 163 people, mostly women and children; some estimate that as many as 400 were slaughtered.

John Dyer was gratified when Chivington invited him to preach, and he soon forgot that he was dressed as a shabby miner.

By the end of March 1862, John Dyer was asked to take charge of the Blue River Mission in Summit County. His circuit would include American Gulch, Breckenridge, Delaware Flats, Galena Gulch, Gold Run, Lincoln City, Mayo Gulch, and Georgia Gulch. (Parkville was the mining camp that grew up at the mouth of Georgia Gulch.) It was, he estimated, a circuit that would stretch two weeks.

The next day, he started walking for the mountains and his circuit.

By the time he reached Georgia Gulch on the second of April, he had only ten cents in his pocket. To help him, the miners there raised $22.50 in gold dust, the prevailing currency at the time.

The Conference would appropriate $125 for his expenses, but this would not cover basic board, which then cost $7 a week.

He bought a small cabin, about 18' x 18', in French Gulch (then called Lincoln City). He furnished it simply, covered the bare dirt floors with gunnysacks, and covered his table with two copies of the *Northwestern Christian Advocate*. He "tried to keep up with the times." He would soon be able to preach to his neighbors in his own home.

John Dyer was a Methodist "of the old stamp," with no tolerance for alcohol and dancing. He remembered a Christmas dinner followed by a dance at the hotel in Lincoln City. After dinner, the ladies in the group invited him to the Christmas dance. When he refused their offer, the lady of the house asked him again, "This is an extra occasion, and it will be no harm for you to dance with me; why can't you accept my offer?"

John Dyer replied, "You're a lady, but not quire handsome enough for me to dance with."

He soon left, spending the night in a cabin about two minutes away. Meanwhile, the crowd danced and drank until dawn, finally moving on to Walker's saloon. Here, they decided to wake the preacher, bring him to the saloon, and have him either treat the drunken crowd or speak on temperance. He needed to go right then and forego breakfast, the crowd insisted. Father Dyer slipped out of his cabin and went to talk with the unruly miners. The drunken miners could not have imagined Father Dyer's response. In control of the mob – he scolded them, as he would reprimand misbehaving children! As he relates in his autobiography:

> *I said: "Gentleman, first I will tell you what I think! There is not a man here but would be ashamed for his father, mother, sisters, or brothers, to know just our condition here this morning." They stamped and roared out, "That's so," all over the house. "and next," I continued, "if we were not so drunk, we would not be here." (Cheers, "That's so, too!" all over the house.) "And if we were a little drunker, we could not do as we are now doing." (Cheers and "That's so!" all over the house.) I wound up and*

was about to tke leave, but the judge said: "I move that we vote that every thing Mr. Dyer has said is true;" and they gave a rousing vote. He said, "The ayes have it," but that I must not go yet; and made a motion that they all give Mr. Dyer one dollar apiece; and that was also carried. They took the hat, got twenty dollars, and I thanked them and went home to breakfast.

Dancing remained an anathema to him:

The evils of balls will never be revealed until the great day of accounts. I used to say that the people must not expect anything from a preacher but opposition to dancing, since John the Baptist lost his head through the flirtations of a silly girl. But I always felt incapable of doing the subject justice.

Even in April, the snow was five feet deep, and travel was difficult. To get around in the mountains, he made a pair of 9 to 11 feet long, Norwegian-style skis, or "snow-shoes" as he called them. He carried a pole to break off clumps of snow sticking to the skis. That spring he learned to ski. In his autobiography Father Dyer recalled learning how to ski:

I made me a pair of snow-shoes, and, of course, was not an expert. Sometimes I would fall; and, on one occasion, as I was going down the mountain to Gold Run, my shoes got crossed in front as I was going very fast. A little pinetree was right in my course, and I could not turn, and dare not encounter the tree with the shoes crossed; and so threw myself into the snow, and went in out of sight.

The following year, in March 1863, he received an official appointment for South Park, a two-week circuit that stretched across Buckskin Joe, Mosquito, Fairplay, and Tarryall. In his autobiogrphy, he told how Mosquito got its name:

The miners met to organize. Several names were suggested, but they disagreed, and a motion was made to adjourn and meet again, the place for the name to be left blank. When they cane together on appointment, the secretary opened the book, and a large mosquito was mashed right in the blank, showed it, and all agreed to call the district Mosquito.

Father Dyer also included California Gulch because no preacher had been assigned to that area. He skied across his circuit, preaching about three or four times a week. While not a minister, he was called "Father Dyer" by a far-flung congregation that loved and respected him.

This appointment settled any indecision he may have had about staying in Colorado. "This decided me to stand the storms and leave the events with God," he declared in his autobiography, "and do the best I could to build up the Church in this wilderness country." In the years to come, he would welcome his sisters, his children, and his widowed father to join him in Colorado.

The summer of 1863 was marked by a widespread drought that dried up the small mountain streams and stunted crops. This was followed by the most severe winter in memory. Heavy snows fell early, blocking supply trains, killing free-range livestock, and delaying stages. Prices for hay, grain, food, and other supplies hit famine prices in Denver and across the Front Range.

Money was always a problem for Father Dyer, even when he lived in Wisconsin and Minnesota. Throughout his autobiography, he remembers the prices he paid and his efforts to save money. He walked thousands of miles to save wagon fares. Some of his frugality can be traced to two major financial panics. When the Panic of 1837 plunged the country into a depression, he was only 25 years old, a husband and father of two young sons. The country had recovered from the panic when it was again thrown into financial chaos by the Panic of 1857. Perhaps it was his frugailty and his fear of financial obligaton that led him to own his own home rather than rent.

To supplement the unpredictable offering plate, he contracted to carry the mail across Mosquito Pass, beginning early February

1864. He carried the mail once a week, skiing the 37 miles from Buckskin Joe across California Gulch to Cache Creek. He earned $18 a week. Carrying the mail across Mosquito Pass in the winter was often harrowing. Winter snows drifted from three to twenty feet deep across the old Indian trail, making the treacherous pass even more difficult when the snow stuck to his skis. Hundreds of travelers who did not have coach fare to Leadville died of exposure trying to walk across this pass, earning it the grisly nickname, "The Highway of Frozen Death."

To his mail route, he added an express business, exchanging gold dust for paper currency. At the time, an ounce of gold dust was worth $40 in paper currency. This profitable sideline added about 5 to 7 pounds to the 23 to 26 pounds of mail that he already carried.

He added another part-time job, working as agent for *The Rocky Mountain News*.

After the first month, other travelers would occasioally ask to accompany Father Dyer across the Mosquito Range. In his autobiogrphy, he recalled a fateful trip:

> *I often went in the night, as it thawed in the day so that it was impossible to travel, and other passengers sought to go with me. A man came up from Denver, and we had a hard trip. He begged me to stop. On top of the range he lay down to sleep, and it was with difficulty that I could get him up. I knew that if he went to sleep, chilled as we were, he would never awake until the judgment. We finally reached Oro City at breakfast-time. That man was one of the leaders of a mob that caused the death of a number of better men than he was. One of his victims was my son.*

On one trip across Mosquito Pass, he suffered a near case of frost-bite on his feet and was fortunate to find his way back to his cabin. He was laid up for two weeks while his feet healed. In his autobiography, he makes a rare reference to Horace Tabor during this period. He "sent to H. A. W. Tabor, our store-keeper -- now ex-senator – and paid him sixteen cents a pound for corn to make hominy, which I considered a luxury."

He carried the mail until August 1864.

On 1 September 1864, his son Elias enlisted as private in Troop I, Colorado 3rd Cavalry. Elias had suffered from "white swelling" when a teenager and walked with a cane, but he could ride a horse. After serving four months, he was mustered out on 31 December 1864 at Denver, Colorado.

Father Dyer encouraged his younger sister Ann, now married to William Bailey, to come to Colorado, and in 1864 they joined an ox train and moved West. With the Baileys came John Dyer's youngest sister, Elizabeth Entriken. She had been pressured by her father to marry an older widower with five children at home, rather than marry the man she loved. Elizabeth relented and married Smith Entriken on 1 May 1860 at Iowa County, Wisconsin. Elizabeth was counted with Smith Entriken (often spelled Entrikin) in the 1860 Census; they had been married within the year. Soon into this loveless marriage, she had a baby, but the infant died. Unhappy in her marriage and mourning her child, she left her husband, joining her sister Ann. She would move to Colorado to begin a new life. John Dyer suggested that the Baileys and his sister, Elizabeth Entriken, settle midway between Buckskin Joe and Denver. He had found a spot with a lush meadow that he thought would be an ideal location for a stagecoach stop. In 1864, William and Ann built a stagecoach station known as Bailey's Ranch and hotel. Eventually, a small town called Bailey grew up near the stagecoach stop.

With his various jobs, Father Dyer was able to save over a thousand dollars. Only a few years before, he had arrived in Denver, deeply in debt, with no cash and no prospects. He could now set aside $800 to pay his debts. With the remaining $300, John Dyer bought eight cows, keeping them on shares with his brother-in-law, William Bailey. With gossip, this small herd of cows grew.

The small herd, he later said in his autobiography, "was used as an excuse to give him a poor appointment; and to excuse the people for not paying his salary."

Father Dyer's youngest son, Samuel, had recently returned home, mustered out on April 1964 after his right foot was amputated. On 30 April 1864, Samuel filed for an Army disability pension, citing his service with the 5th Wisconsin Infantry.

That summer, Indians threatened the settlers. Father Dyer recalled that "the Indians were on the Plains, and there was no traveling without guards, and no mail for almost three months." These Indian uprisings forced the Methodist conference, scheduled for that summer, to be postponed until fall.

THE CIVIL WAR

John Dyer was acting chairman for the Methodist conference, held the fall of 1864 in Central City. John Dyer's circuit for the upcoming year had expanded. It now included South Park, as well as Oro City (now, Leadville), Colorado City, Canon City, Pueblo, and stretched south to Trinidad. He briefly visited New Mexico the following spring.

At the next conference held the summer of 1865 in Denver, he urged Bishop Kingsley to appoint a missionary to the New Mexico district who could teach the Spanish. Father Dyer took ten conference attendees, including Bishop Kingsley, to a photography studio for a group picture that cost $25.

In the photograph (below), Father Dyer is seated second from the left in the front row. Attendees pictured standing in the top row, from the left, are: C.H. Kirkbride, George Richardson, William Antes, W.W. Baldwin, R.T. Vincent, John Gilliland, and G.T. McMains. In the front row, seated from the left, are G.A. Willard, Father Dyer, Bishop Calvin Kingsley, and Charles King. When Father Dyer wrote his autobiography, he fondly recalled the conference and "thinks more of the picture now than he ever thought he would."

Photograph (modified) of 1865 Conference Attendees, from *Echoes from Peak to Plain* (1898) by Isaac Haight Beardsley.

It was 1865, the final, most desperate year of the Civil War.

John Dyer worried about his oldest son, Joshua, who had enlisted with the 1st Minnesota Infantry. Joshua had been captured at the Battle of Petersburg in Virginia on 28 June 1864 and was being held as a prisoner of war. The last he had heard, Joshua, sick and nearly starving, had been sent from Wilmington, North Carolina, to the infamous Andersonville Prison. He had been part of a prisoner exchnge program and would be exchanged soon. He thought his son was dead, but the uncertainty grew. He grappled with the faint possibility that he might be able to do something, that possibly his son was alive.

In December 1865, he decided to go back East to settle matters. He could wait no longer. He needed to know.

Indian uprisings and attacks on wagon trains had escalated. To start across the plains, a wagon train was required to have at least 40 armed men. As he prepared for his trip, John Dyer bought a rifle and a handgun that he hoped he would never need to use. He was fortunate, and instead of soldiering, he ministered to the sick along the way. When they reached Fort Kearney, he negotiated to join a light carriage to Nebraska City. Here, his pistol was stolen, but he still had his rifle. He made his way to Fall City, where he met with his brother, Thomas Dyer. He then went to Lenora, Minnesota, where he met with Charles Streeter, his daughter's husband. Still, there was no word. . . until they received a letter from a friend, listing the names of all soldiers aboard the ill-fated *General Lyon,* the ship carrying Union soldiers in the prisoner exchange program. The steamship had blown up off the coast of Cape Hatteras, and all aboard had been lost. John Dyer was devastated when he read his son's name on the passenger list. Joshua's body was never recovered.

Still, the question of Joshua's death lingered, the fading hope of a desolate father. Joshua's body was never recovered . . . .

Father Dyer continued his Eastern trip, visiting Boston, New York City, Baltimore, Washington, and Philadelphia. He had never been farther east than Ohio, and he needed a break. Perhaps travel and new sights would help. In April 1866, he returned to Colorado and his preaching in the mountains. He had no interest in ever visiting the East again.

The next month, on 18 May 1866, Joshua's widow, Lucy Charlotte (Mosher) Dyer, filed for an Army pension, citing Joshua's service as sergeant, Company B, 1st Minnesota Infantry They had been married on 17 February 1864 at Argyle, Minnesora.

In 1867, Father Dyer was elected Lake County probate judge, resigning about a year later when he was assigned to the New Mexico District.

In 1868, Father Dyer fulfilled his dream of building a church. He paid $100 for a two-storey log building in Montgomery that had once been a hotel. He then had it hauled from Montgomery to Fairplay for another $100. Once the structure was in place, Father Dyer and Brother Warren spent a month finishing the interior of the 40' x 24' building. They partitioned the last 14 feet for a temporary parsonage for Brother Warren and his wife.

In his autobiography, Father Dyer recalled how much Brother Warren wanted to have a revival in the new church. When he asked Father Dyer how many he could expect, Father Dyer responded, "Three." Brother Warren responded that he "could not ask the Lord for less than twenty." "But," mused Father Dyer in his autobiography, "he did not then know the Rocky Mountain sinners as he did afterwards." Brother Warren stayed for two years, often fighting cruel gossip and harassment. "The roughs," Father Dyer reported, "went so far as to shave his horse."

Isaac Beardsley (*Echoes from Peak and Plain,* 1898) recorded an example of Father Dyer's caustic wit:

> *Some time during the early spring of 1868, one Sabbath afternoon, weary and dusty from a walk of over a hundred miles, he met with the old Lawrence Street Sunday-school, when the pastor made the following announcement: "Children, Old Father Dyer is in the audience, and after singing this hymn he will make a short talk." The hymn was sung, and the pastor invited "Old Father Dyer" forward to the altar to address the school.*

> *This reference quickened his pulse, as he walked upon the platform with a firm and elastic step, and with a peculiar twinkle in one corner of his eye, in a drawling tone of voice, he began with: "O-l-d F-a-t-h-e-r D-y-e-r; yes, children, O-l-d F-a-t-h-e-r D-y-e-r. I may be old; but I am not barefoot on the top of my head, neither do I wear store teeth tied into my mouth with a string!"*

> *The point of the joke will readily be seen, when we recollect that, although their pastor was about twenty-two years younger than he, yet the top of his head was "above timber-line," and he wore false teeth.*

Chosen a delegate to the General Conference in Chicago, Father Dyer left Denver, taking five days to reach Coyote, arriving about

1:45 in the morning. He

> *called at several tents, asking for some kind of a bed, At last a man said if I could sleep with two others in a bed, I could come in. I lodged with them till about daylight, when I discovered it was a saloon. He charged me a dollar; and I found a restaurant, and paid a dollar for breakfast.*

From near Coyote, he caught a train East. He visited his father at Pleasant Hill, Missouri. In his autobiography, he wrote that he traveled from St. Louis

> *to Illinois, Wisconsin, and Minnesota. My daughter lived in Minnesota, and at Juda in Wisconsin my son was keeping a drug-store. So I had quite a visit, take it all around.*

At the next quarterly meeting held in Golden, Colorado, Father Dyer was assigned to the New Mexico District in 1869. He tried to refuse the appointment "on the ground of nonadaptability," but he was chosen anyway (Beardsley, 1898). "This appointment," he recalled in his autobiography, "was not taken without at least some knowledge of the labor, privation, and dangers attending a protestant preacher in that field." Father Dyer would be leaving his sons, his daughter, his father. He would leave behind nearly everything he depended on for a living. He deeded to his son his half-interest in the Hayden Ranch, packed a pony, and left for his life in New Mexico.

He soon settled in a fast-growing mining town, Elizabethtown, New Mexico. He was a miner himself and would be comfortable preaching to the miners here. In his autobiography written twenty years later, John Dyer spoke fondly of the miners:

> *Often after preaching I was greeted warmly, and some of them [the miners] would say the service reminded them of home. They were generally liberal, although it was not the custom always to pass the hat, and sometimes the preacher, when his pants began to wear out, would think the boys rather long be-*

tween collections. It was common to give a dollar all around; and to this day I would as soon ask miners for help, with assurance of receiving, as any class of men I have ever found. They were always ready to divide, although at times they would take exceptions to a man that wore a plug hat or noticeably fine clothes.

Like many gold mining boom towns, Elizabethtown exploded when gold was found, quickly fizzled when the gold played out, and was soon abandoned, a derelict ghost town. Founded only a few years earlier in 1866, Elizabethtown's population grew to about 7,000 by 1870, but as the mines played out, nearly everyone left. By 1872, there were only 100 people left in Elizabethtown, the first incorporated town in New Mexico.

Father Dyer headquarted in Santa Fe, preaching at Albuquerque, Fort Craig, Fort Selden, Las Cruces, Masea, and Soccoro, despite Indian scares and danger from robbers and killers. After returning to Santa Fe, he went to Elizabethtown, Cimarron, Red River, and La Junta. He preached wherever he could find listeners, whether in town or in a cattleherders' camp. He later estimated that he had traveled "ten thousand miles on horseback in two years."

Father Dyer filed for land under the Homestead Act of 1862 in Douglas County, Colorado, entry #1871 dated 17 January 1871. His son Samuel also filed, entry #2169 in Douglas County dated 17 July 1871. The Homestead Act, a boon to Colorado's agriculture, enabled any citizen 21 years old or the head of a family to acquire 160 acres of land.

The summer 1870 Conference was at Pueblo, Colorado. Father Dyer was now assigned to the Divide Circuit, a four-week's travel and preaching circuit south and east of Denver.

By the time the 1870 Census was taken, Elizabeth was living with her sister Ann and her sister's husband, William Bailey,

Following the death of his wife Cassandra in 1869, Samuel Dyer had moved west to Colorado to be with his children, John, Elizabeth, and Ann, and his grandchildren. He settled in Bailey, Colorado, where he died 28 November 1871. He was initially buried at Bailey, Colorado, and later reburied by his son, Father Dyer, in the Dyer family plot at Cedar Hill Cemetery in Castle Rock, Colorado.

On 7 November 1870, Father Dyer married Mrs. Lucinda (Lord) Rankin, the widow of Joseph Rankin, at Denver, Colorado. As he explained in his autobiography,

> *I had been a widower over twenty years, and had never seen the time that I thought I could live and support a family without locating. But since I could almost keep myself, I thought it was a poor woman who could not help a little. So we were married, and, by God's blessing, lived happily together until she was called to her reward.*

Father Dyer lamented the lawlessness he found in the the district south and east of Denver.

> *The settlers were ranchmen. Stock was ranging far away, and the loss of a cow was more seriously felt than that of a human being. If a man were killed, it was looked over, and the murderer allowed to escape justice. (When Father Dyer published his autobiography in 1890, he was still pained by the 1875 murder of his son Elias at the hands of a criminal mob.) But if a man stole cattle, he was almost sure, if caught, to be hung. Trial by court was too slow and uncertain.*

At the 1874 Methodist conference, Father Dyer was apponted to the newly-settled Monument Circuit. Here, there was no house. While living in the rear of a bowling alley for about a month, he built a snall house, about 16' x 24', He was also able to build a stable for his ponies and a cow. He was frugal, and when he was finished, he and Lucinda were comfortable in their new parsonage. And, they were not in debt, an ever-present worry.

THE MURDER OF JUDGE ELIAS DYER

On 3 July 1875, Judge Elias Dyer, Father Dyer's middle son, was murdered in his courtroom in what later became known as the Lake County War, an era marked by vigilante justice and violence. Father Dyer was devastated, and the pain was still sharp when he wrote his autobiography 15 years later,

> *A strange fascination holds me to this dreadful scene. No wonder. My son, educated, bright, wayward it may be, but honest and fearless – to have been so wickedly torn away from me! O, the weary, weary months of anquish; the alternate flashes of revenge and forgiveness; the bitter struggles between wrath and mercy! God have pity! – even now, when I retrace the efforts to traduce his character, made by his cowardly murderers, my old blood boils! My son was not perfect; but his sins were against himself, and his last letters show how his better nature was dominating.*

The Lake County War had begun a year earlier when George Harrington, a Lake County homesteader, had an ongoing conflict with his neighbor, Elijah Gibbs, over rights to a drainage ditch.

In the early morning of 17 June 1874, George Harrington was surprised by a mob that had set fire to one of his outbuildings. When he and his wife tried to extinguish the flames, he was fatally shot in the back. Because of their ongoing feud, Elijah Gibbs was the prime suspect in the murder.

That fall, Elijah Gibbs and Stuart McClish were acquitted of Harrington's murder by a Denver court, which ruled the shooting was in self defense. The venue had been changed to Denver because the case was so emotionally charged.

The *Colorado Daily Chieftan* on 10 November 1874 reported the acquittal:

> *Elijah Gibbs and Stuart McClish, recently tried at Denver for the murder of Geo. Harrington, on Gas Creek, Lake county, were acquitted. The evdence against them was of the flimsiest character.*

Gibbs returned to his home as though nothing had happened, but Harrington's friends could not accept the verdict. They took justice in their own hands.

On 22 January 1875, a drunken posse of about 15 of Harrington's friends went to Gibb's cabin, demanding that he come out to be lynched. They tried to set fire to the cabin, but even with kindling, the logs were too wet. From inside his cabin, Gibbs shot at the mob trying to set his home ablaze, killing two men. A third man soon died from a misfired rifle. Gibbs later turned himself in to the local justice of the peace. At trial the next day, the court found that Gibbs had acted in self defense, and he immediately fled the area.

With Gibbs now gone, Harrington's friends formed the "Committee of Safety," to interrogate Gibb's friends and supporters. In a mock trial, the committee would loop a noose around the neck of a witness, tightening the noose if the witness did not say what the vigilantes wanted to hear.

Judge Elias Dyer swore out arrest warrants for 16 members of the Committee of Safety.

The details of the assassination were reported on the front page of *The Rocky Mountain News* on 6 July 1875.

ANOTHER "REIGN OF TERROR."
Murder of a Probate Judge by the

Sheriff of Lake County and the
So-called Committee of Safety
Particulars of the Tragedy

[Special to the News]

FAIRPLAY, July 5. –This place is the scene of terrible excitement over a tragedy that, used as all are here to deeds of blood, strikes the entire community with a horror not felt for many a long day. The feud which has divided Lake county into two factions, each equally lawless, although one purporting to be the representative of order and legal authority, ever since the shooting of Harrington by Elisha Gibbs over a year ago, which resulted in the night attack on Gibbs' house on the 22nd of last January to the mortal harm of two of the assailants, and the final running of Gibbs out of the country, has culminated in the murder of Judge Dyer, of the probate court of this county for no other crime, apparently, than endeavoring to do his duty. The particulars, as near as I have been able to collect them, are as follows: Dyer had issued sixteen warrants for the arrest of members of the so-called Committee of Safety, and deputized Doctor Dobbins to arrest them. The latter returned the warrants, saying he had showed them to one Burnett, but had no means of bringing him to Granite. Dyer then deputized a man named Sites, who proceeded to carry out the order. He went immediately to Brown creek and arrested first, Burnett, and afterwards, Chaffin, a ring leader of the Safety Committee faction, and a man named Moore. Sites then went up the river to make other arrests, and on returning to Brown creek met Welden (sic - Weldon), the sheriff of Lake county, who told him to give him the warrants, as he could make more arrests in one day than he (Sites) could in three weeks. Sites gave him the warrants, and last Friday evening the sheriff of Lake county, with about thirty armed men, came to Granite a little before dark. The mob took Dyer to the court room. Fifteen or twenty citizens followed, but were ordered back. What transpired in the court room no one knows. When Dyer came out he was very pale. He immediately went to Johnson's store and wrote a letter. That night he was guarded, and the next morning the mob again took him to the court house. A few moments after entering they came out; but shortly afterwards they returned and, as they were passing up the stairs, four shots were fired. One ball struck Dyer on the arm. When he found himself wounded, he begged for his life, but the assassins finished him by shooting him in the head at the back of the right ear, the ball lodging beneath the left eye brow [sic]. He lived fifteen minutes and was conscious but unable to speak. While Dyer lay weltering in his blood and in the death agony, John D. Coon, a ring-leader of the mob, bent over him exclaiming: "What a horrible murder," which sentiment is reechoed by the men hereabouts who are aching to hang Mr. Coon for his share in the crime. I will endeavor to collect further details of subsequent occurences [sic] as I shall be able to gather them, but do so at the peril of my life, if any of the committee of safety learn of my taking such action.

Knowing that he would be murdered by the Committee of Safety, Judge Dyer wrote a letter to his father, which Father Dyer included in his autobiography:

Granite, July 3, 1875
Dear Father, – I do n't know that the sun will ever rise and set for me again, but I trust in God and his mercy. At eight o'clock I sit in court. The mob have me under guard. Mr. Gilland is missing this morning, but I do not think harm has befallen him..God bless you, my father in your old age, and in Sam and his boy – in all your children – but you know John bears the name (Samuel's son, John Lewis Dyer, was named for Father Dyer). Bless him and his forever, O my God.

My love to all friends, and I say I am proud to be your son. There is no cowardice in me, father. I am worthy of you in this respect. God comfort you and keep you always. I am, in this one respect, like Him who died for all; I die, if die I must, for law, order, and principle; and, too, I stand alone.

Your loving and true, and, I hope in some respects, worthy son,

Elias F. Dyer

Father Dyer tried to get Governor Routt to intervene, but the governor would not listen. No arrests were ever made in Judge Dyer's murder. As many as 100 people may have been killed in the Lake County War before violence waned about 1881. In his autobiography Father Dyer recalled his pain:

God only knows how hard a trial this terrible tragedy was to me. After the lapse of all these years, the memory of it rushes over me like a flood. Yet I would infinitely rather endure my suffering than what his cruel murderers must have experienced. One was so crazed that he drowned himself. Another had what was called the "horrors," and finally miserably died. God's curse was upon them all. Be it so!

After the death of his son, Father Dyer sold Elias' half interest in his son's poorly-performing mine to Horace Tabor for $3,000. Two years later, the half interest resold for $60,000.

PREACHING ACROSS THE MOUNTAINS

On 1 August 1876, Colorado was finally accepted into the Union, making it the 38th state. It had been a long struggle, but Colorado was finally a state, the Centennial State.

The 1876 Conference was at Boulder, Colorado, and Father Dyer was assigned to Fairplay and Alma, a high mountain town founded in 1861. He fought deep blinding snows to preach at the Dolly Varden mine, where he was well received. The next day he preached to 60 miners at the Moose mine, and later the Australia mine, before returning to Fairplay. For the rest of the year, he preached across Park County almost four times a week.

On 8 June 1877, Rusha (Thurston) Dyer died. She was the first wife of Father Dyer's only surviving son, Samuel. She was buried with other Dyer family members at Cedar Hill Cemetery in Castle Rock. Samuel was now a widowed invalid with a four-year-old son, Father Dyer's namesake, John Lewis Dyer, born on 13 January 1873.

Father Dyer was appointed a supernumerary at the 1877 Conference, and two years later at the conference in Pueblo was appointed to the Breckenridge Circuit. He had been at the circuit for a month when Utes attacked the Indian agency at the White River Ute Reservation, killing Indian agent Nathan Meeker and ten of his employees, and kidnapping Meeker's wife and daughter. Known as the Meeker Massacre, this attack triggered the Ute War. Many terrified residents fled. Fake news reached Governor Pitkin that the Utes had attacked Breckenridge and left it in ashes. The panic was a rumor-fed scare, and there were no Indians within a hundred miles. Soon, the sheepish residents returned.

It was not long before Bresckenridge was again awash in excitement. . . this time because of its own gold rush. When word circulated that gold quartz and carbonates had been found near Breckenridge, it triggered a gold rush. Father Dyer recalled how the lure of gold brought people from

> *across the range, and of course, the inevitable dancehouse, with degraded women, fiddles, bugles, and many sorts of music, came too. There was a general hubbub from dark to daylight. The weary could hardly rest. Claims were staked out everywhere, amd the prospector thought nothing of shoveling five feet of snow to start a shaft. Saloons, grocery-stores, carpenter-shops, and every kind of business sprang up, ncluding stamp-mills and smelters. All classes were excited beyond all good sense. Town-lots, that could have been bought before at twenty-give to fifty dollars, brought fifteen hundred dollars. Corrals, log-heaps, and brush-thickets were all turned into town-lots.Those owning ground thought it worth ten times more than it was. The excitement was almost as great as when they thought the Indians were coming.*

That fall, Father Dyer bought a cabin on a lot about 150' x 50'. After a boundary dispute with the Breckenridge Town Company, in which he could lose about a third of his property, he donated half his lot to the trustees to build a church. He recalled building the church:

> *We carried a subscription paper till I got enough to start on; and went to the saw-mills, got all the lumber I could, and we went to work and put up a house twenty-five by fifty feet, posts sixteen feet high, and inclosed it. I nailed the first shingle, and did more work on it than any other man.*

Father Dyer estimated that the church, including the lot, cost him about $350. Over time, the church has been relocated and enlarged, and today welcomes both members and visitors.

The 1880 conference was in Georgetown. By the time Father Dyer returned to Breckenridge, the site of a gold rush the prior year, he found that the excitement had died down, and lot prices crashed to pre-boom prices. As quickly as the gold fever descended on Breckenridge, it left just as quickly.

This was a poor assignment for Father Dyer, but he supplemented his salary with temporary jobs and was well paid for locating claims, reportedly by dowsing for them. Also, his wife Lucinda helped by taking in boarders. When the census was taken that year, Father Dyer and Lucinda had a boarder, John Parkinson, living with them in their home on Ridge Street in Breckenridge, Colorado. Their neighbors included miners, bakers, grocers, the town marshal, and others drawn to a growing community.

In 1880, Father Dyer's son Samuel was a widowed druggist living at a hotel in Castle Rock, Colorado, about a hunded miles from Breckenridge. Samuel married (2) Esther Alexander on 2 June 1881.

In January 1881, Father Dyer started bulding a home about six miles outside of Breckenridge and about a half mile from the Warrior's Mark mine, in which he had a stake. By 19 February 1881, he moved into the home with his wife Lucinda. It had taken him less than two months to build the 17'x 17' storey-and-a-half log home. Over time, a small town – Dyersville -- grew up near Father Dyer's cabin, settled by miners who worked at the nearby Warrior's Mark mine. After working the Warrior's Mark mine for a year or two, Father Dyer sold his interest in the mine for $2,000. Today, Dyersville is a ghost town dotted with remnants of log cabins and can be reached with a four-wheel drive vehicle.

At the next Conference, he was appointed to the Summit County District, and in December they moved to Father Dyer's Douglas County ranch. By now, he was nearly 70 years old, and he discovered that the physical labor needed to run the ranch was too demanding. After two years, Father Dyer traded the ranch for a home in Denver. In November 1885, Father Dyer and Lucinda moved to 712 Glenarm Street in Denver, near the Colorado State Capitol. He was now 73 years old. He successfully applied for a position as the first Colorado Senate chaplin, It was, Father Dyer recalled in his autobiogralhy, "not lucrative."

He soon visited Breckenridge and was disappointed to find that there was no minister in the church he had founded years before. He told the congregation that he would preach temporarily until a new minister was assigned. In the end, Father Dyer was there for two years. He recalled in his autobiography how he had rescued the church organ from being taken to provide the music for a community dance. Father Dyer was shocked that the mob would even consider taking the organ from the church, the church he had built, for something as profane as a dance!

Lucinda died on 9 April 1888 at the age of 61 at Denver, Colorado. She was buried at Cedar Hill Cemetery in Castle Rock, Colorado.

After Lucinda's death, Father Dyer moved to Deer Valley where he lived with his daughter Abbie and her husband. By the time the 1900 Federal Census was taken, Father Dyer was an 88-year-old widower living with his daughter Elizabeth ("Abbie") and son-in-law, Charles Streeter, at Deer Valley. Colorado. John reported that he was a Methodist preacher, but he hadn't worked during the past 12 months.

Living nearby was his younger sister, Elizabeth Entriken, a 70-year-old boardinghouse keeper. Elizabeth reported that she was a widow who had one child, but the child was no longer living. Elizabeth lived alone in the mountains and never felt the need to lock her doors. Today, Elizabeth's humble cabin, one of the first homesteads in the area, is an historic site designated on the Colorado state register. It has been moved a short distance to McGraw Memorial Park, where it is open to the public. *The Denver Post* (5 May 1922) sketched the independence and unflappability of this remarkable pioneer woman:

One day Chief Colorow and a dozen of his braves rode their ponies up to her door and gruffly demanded biscuits. She motioned them to the table and baked two large pans full. They fell upon them hungrily and grunted for more. This performance was repeated time after time. No sooner would she bring in fresh pans and her back be turned than the biscuits would vanish. After she had baked for nearly an hour and her flour barrel was sadly depleted, she became indignant and firmly shook her head at Colorow, a huge figure in a white "boiled shirt" some storekeeper had given him, despairing of ever having a call for such a freakish large size.

Refuses to Bake Any More Biscuits.

"No more, no more," she said. "You're eating me out of house and home. Not another biscuit do you get."

Colorow growled and repeated, "Hungry; hurry!" She informed him curtly that she had no more flour to spare, her barrel was almost empty.

In endeavoring to mount his pony the front of the "boiled shirt" came out of Colorow's trousers and there fell to the ground a cascade of biscuits. She looked at the other braves and noticed how their bodies also resembled barrels.

"For a moment I was mad clear thru, to think how they had been 'stuffing' away my biscuits," Mrs. Entriken would relate. "Then I had an almost irresistible desire to laugh. But I kept a grave face, told Colorow to remain on this horse and picked up for him the biscuits he had dropped. He never even thanked me, but calmly stuffed them back into his shirt. However, he never again tried that trick. He was grateful that I saved his dignity, came several times and ate biscuits and told me I was a 'heap good squaw' and his friend. None of the Utes ever bothered me, not even afterward when the Indians grew ugly and the Colorado militia was ordered out against them."

Son Samuel, now a 50-year-old miner, was living with his second wife, Esther, at Cripple Creek, Colorado, in 1900. The household included Samuel's step-daughter and four lodgers.

The new Colorado State Capitol Building was completed and opened to the public in 1901. Designed by Elijah E. Myers, it featured stained glass windows in the rotunda – a "circle of fame" honoring sixteen people who had significantly contributed to the history of Colorado. Father Dyer was one of those sixteen.

After a lingering illness, Father Dyer died from paralysis of the throat on 16 June 1901 in Denver, Colorado. He was 89 years old. He was buried near other family members at Cedar Hill Cemetery in Castle Rock, Colorado.

The Coshocton (Ohio) Daily Age was one of many newpapers that reported Father Dyer's death on the front page on 17 June 1901:

The Snowshoe Itinerant.

Denver, 17. - the Rev. John L. Dyer, one of the most famous preachers who has figured in the history of the west, died of paralysis of the throat after a lingering illness. Mr. Dyer was born in Franklin county, O, in 1812. "Father" Dyer, as he beame known, began preaching in Wisconsin in 1849, and was the oldest, if not the last of the old Methodist "circuit riders." Coming to Colorado in 1861 he met many thrilling adventures in his travels in this state and New Mexico, and through his zeal in preaching to the widely separated and almost inaccessible mining camps in all kinds of weather earned the sobriquet "The Snowshoe Itinerant." He is the author of a book bearing that title.

Father Dyer was one of the last circuit riders, and with his passing he beame a Colorado legend, an outspoken, prospecting, skiing, preacher who sacrificed much to bring the Gospel to the mountains.

Two Rocky Mountain peaks, both 13ers, are named in Father

Dyer's honor: Dyer Mountain, 13,862 ft. elevation, in the Mosquito Range about 10 miles east of Leadville, and Father Dyer Peak, 13,622 ft. elevation, in Tenmile Range.

In 1977, Father Dyer was posthumously inducted into the Colorado Ski and Snowboard Hall of Fame.

BIBLIOGRAPHY

Anderson, Fred. *Crucible of War. The Seven Years' War and the Fate of Empire in British North America, 1754-1766.* New York: Alfred A. Knopf, 2000.

Beardsley, Isaac Haight. *Echoes from Peak and Plain, or Tales of Life, War, Travel and Colorado Methodism.* Cincinnati: Curts & Jennings, 1898.

J. C. B. *Travels in New France by J. C. B.,* ed. Sylvester K. Stevens, et. al., eds. Harrisburg: The Pennsylvania Historical Commission, 1941.

Baker-Crothers. Hayes. *Virginia in the French and Indian War.* Chicago: University of Chicago Press, 1928. This book was reprinted by Heritage Books, Inc. in 2007.

Crofutt, Geo. A. *Crofutt's Grip-Sack Guide of Colorado.* Omaha: The Overland Publishing Co., 1885.

Dyer, John L[ewis]. *The Snow-Shoe Itinerant, An Autobiography of the Rev. John L. Dyer, Familiarly known as "Father Dyer" of the Colorado Conference, Methodist Episcopal.* Cincinnati: Cranston and Stowe, 1890.

Hall, Frank. History of the State of Colorado. Volume I. Published for the Rocky Mountain Historical Society. Chicago: The Blakely Printing Company, 1889.

Harwood, Rev. Thomas. *History of New Mexico Spanish and English Missions of the Methodist Episcopal Church from 1850 to 1910. Volume II.* Albuquerque: El Abogado Press, 1910.

Kile, Robin Propst. *Hidden in the Mountains: Fort Seybert 1758.* Blomington, Indiana: Life-Rich Publishing, 2017.

Morton, Oren F. *A History of Pendleton County, West Virginia.* Dayton, Virginia: Ruebush-Elkins Co., 1910.

Talbot, Mary Lee Keister. *The Dyer Settlement; The Ft. Seybert Massacre.* Chicago: Larson-Dingle Printing Co., 1937.

Wickersheim, Laurel, and Rawlene LeBaron. *The Lost Cities of Colorado.* Maryland: Heritage Books, Inc., 2002.

-----------------------. *Mine Owners and Mines of the Colorado Gold Rush.* Maryland: Heritage Books, Inc., 2006.

-----------------------. *Colorado on the Eve of Statehood: An Edited Business Directory of the Pioneers who Built the Centennial State.* Maryland: Heritage Books, Inc., 2008.

Willison, George F. *Here They Dug the Gold.* New York: Reynal & Hitchcock, 1946.